Elvis!
The Last Word

ELVIS!
The
Last
Word

by
Sandra Choron
and
Bob Oskam

The 328 Best (and Worst) Things Anyone Ever Said About "The King"

A Citadel Press Book
Published by Carol Publishing Group

A Citadel Press Book
Published by Carol Publishing Group
Citadel Press is a registered trademark of Carol Communications, Inc.

Editorial Offices: 600 Madison Avenue, New York, N.Y. 10022
Sales & Distribution Offices: 120 Enterprise Avenue, Secaucus, N.J. 07094
In Canada: Musson Book Company, a division of General Publishing Co., Ltd.,
    Don Mills, Ontario   M3B 2T6

Queries regarding rights and permissions should be addressed to Carol Publishing Group, 600 Madison Avenue, New York, N.Y. 10022

Carol Publishing Group books are available at special discounts for bulk purchases, for sales promotions, fund raising, or educational purposes. Special editions can be created to specifications. For details contact: Special Sales Department, Carol Publishing Group, 120 Enterprise Avenue, Secaucus, N.J. 07094

Manufactured in the United States of America

10   9   8   7   6   5   4   3   2   1

Library of Congress Cataloging-in-Publication Data

Elvis! : the last word : the man, the myth, the king, in the words of
  his subjects / edited by Sandra Choron and Bob Oskam.
      p.   cm.
    "A Citadel Press book."
    ISBN 0-8065-1280-6
    1. Presley, Elvis, 1935-1977—Quotations.   I. Choron, Sandra.
  II. Oskam, Bob.
  ML420.P96E37   1991
  782.42166'092—dc20
  [B]   91-26912
                                                            CIP
                                                            MN

Photo credits: pp. 21, 49—used with permission by Movie Star News 134 West 18th Street, New York, N.Y. 10011 Phone: (212) 620-8160-61

Quotations from Elvis's high school mates and teachers are reprinted from *Early Elvis: The Humes Years,* by Bill E. Burk, courtesy of Burk Enterprises, Box 16792, Memphis, Tenn. 38186.

Quotations from *Elvis After Life,* by Raymond A. Moody, Jr. (Atlanta, Ga.: Peachtree Publishers, Ltd.) © 1987 by Raymond A. Moody, Jr. Used by permission of the publisher.

To Absent Friends

Contents

Introduction

Suppose you were asked to name the greatest "legend" of twentieth-century America. Who would that be?

No doubt, a whole group of eligible candidates come to mind—Franklin Roosevelt, Albert Einstein, Helen Keller, John D. Rockefeller, Martin Luther King, Jr., Bette Davis, and scores of other politicians, scientists, social reformers, and entertainers.

Okay now, what would you say to this: Elvis Aron Presley is unquestionably the greatest of them all.

"Get serious!" you say. And the considered arguments: "You can't possibly think Elvis had more of an influence on America than someone like Martin Luther King. There's no way Elvis and his music affected society more than the struggle for civil rights in the sixties."

Sure, Elvis was a phenomenon, but to rank him at the top of the list? Come on! How could anyone rate Elvis above those others?

Well, we don't cede an issue when the facts are in our favor. Plus we're precise in our use of terms.

Remember, we're talking legends. That means people who in—and beyond—their lifetime so excited the public imagination that they became mythic figures. Elvis was not just one among many. He was—and remains—one of a kind.

Think of the controversy he generated simply through the act of being himself. Think of the immediate impact he had on everyday behavior—on what was considered proper behavior. Elvis epitomized the conflicts and changes affecting American society. In many respects, he was the one who made the sixties possible. He helped to move us from complacency to self-exploration—and to self-doubt. It was the energized young Elvis who convinced us there was a vital substitute for white bread and the puritanical myth of Norman Rockwell's America. And it was his tragic death that frightened us with stark reality—that self-expression can lead to self-destruction.

We haven't been the same since Elvis. He defined an era. He was America—the fresh young outsider who shook up the system, the shining star with clay feet, and the dissipated innocent who could not understand what he had become. That is the stuff of legends. He set the example that led us to throw off the chains of convention. He reflected our own fatal fascination with being the biggest and the best, and his passing highlighted our loss of control somewhere along the line.

Elvis is the archetypal twentieth-century tragic hero, a distillation of the collective we, the people. Greil Marcus said it particularly well: "The question of Elvis Presley remains as alive as the man himself is dead. He remains the specter of possibility—in rock and roll, pop culture, America, modern life—and he remains the fact of ruin. Solve that question if you can...or else drop the question of who you are, where you came from, and where you might end up."

A whole generation of Americans defined itself in the attitude taken toward Elvis Presley. The issue wasn't whether you liked him or not—the dislike he generated is as much a part of the legend as the adulation. The point is that by declaring your position on Elvis, you identified yourself as either rebel or reactionary, exuberant participant in a newly unleashed social revolution or staunch defender of the status quo. His metamorphosis over the course of three decades from iconoclast to icon reflect both the extent to which the social revolution prevailed and the extent to which it was compromised.

This book documents a transformation. Readers will observe the evolution of a myth, the weaving of legend around a prototypical individual who, whether by a power of his own or in powerless subjection to Fate, was an irresistible agent of change.

This is not an attempt at biography. The details of Elvis's life are sufficiently established elsewhere. They form the matrix through which his legend weaves. The quotes and anecdotes here are threads of the legend itself—pronouncements of significance, parables and fables, testimonies documenting influence. They are both substance and embellishment, accretions to the story of a life that is already a part of the public domain. The quotations are presented in a very rough chronology that is now and again broken in order to juxtapose complementary or conflicting observations, to put a spin on a previous or following item, or simply because a legend does not always submit to chronology.

This kaleidoscope of recollections and impressions does not give us a clear picture of Elvis Aron Presley, the man. Any clarity is but momentary. What we do obtain is an image of presence rather than sharp definition. But that is the nature of legend—a figure who is not just our inspiration but also our invention. As Bruce Springsteen put it, "It was like he came along and whispered a dream in everybody's ear and then we dreamed it."

These fragments of comment and recall are in many respects dream images. Like dreams, they are not so much objective records as multifaceted reflections of our own psyche. This is not simply a book about Elvis—it is a book about us.

The question of Elvis Presley remains as alive as the man himself is dead. He remains the specter of possibility—in rock & roll, pop culture, "America", modern life—and he remains the fact of ruin. Solve that question if you can, say the specter and the fact—or else drop the question of who you are, where you came from, and where you might end up.

—Greil Marcus, rock critic

♪

Presley's importance to rock cannot be overstated. He was the first, he inspired hundreds of others who in turn inspired thousands more. He was there at the birth of—if not responsible for—youth culture. Few artists—in any field—have left such a lasting impression on their times.

—From the entry for Elvis Presley in
The Illustrated Encyclopedia of Rock

♪

There have been a lotta tough guys. There have been pretenders. There have been contenders. But there is only one king.

—Bruce Springsteen

♪

He never really died and never will. You don't change as much of the world as Elvis Presley changed—hair styles, clothes, mood, looks, sideburns—dad gum! He cut a path through the world! He's gonna be history, man.

—Carl Perkins

♪

Elvis Presley was a weapon of the American psychological war aimed at inflicting a part of the population with a new philosophical outlook of inhumanity...to destroy anything that is beautiful in order to prepare for war.

—*Youth World,* an East German
Communist newspaper

Elvis!
The Last Word

...The third happened to take hold of the elephant's trunk. "Both of you are wrong," he said. "Anybody who knows anything can see that this elephant is like a snake."

The fourth reached out his arms and grasped one of the elephant's legs. "Oh, how blind you are! It is very plain to me that he is round and tall like a tree."

The fifth was a very tall man, and he chanced to take hold of the elephant's ear. "The blindest man ought to know that this beast is not like any of the things you name," he said....

—from "The Blind Men and the Elephant," an old Indian folk tale

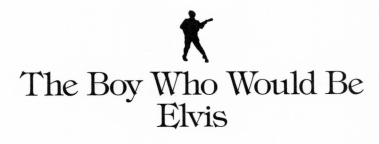

The Boy Who Would Be Elvis

Gladys holds her precious son to her. She has two men in her life now who will depend on her and she on them, and as she looks into the eyes of her devoted husband, she whispers the name of their beloved son that God has chosen for them, Elvis Aaron Presley.

—Vester Presley, Elvis's Uncle, on his birth

Elvis was NOT a mama's boy!...He didn't ever go out looking for trouble, but I never saw Elvis lose a fight.

—Buzzy Forbes, high school mate

Elvis cried for days.

—Gladys Presley, recalling his reaction to the death of a pet chicken.

In one of our classes, he was sitting in the back row and I was sitting a couple of rows in front of him. He would throw wadded up gum wrapper foil at me to get my attention.

—Georgia Avgeris Scarmoutsos, high school mate

[Elvis] came to my office...and told me he was quitting the team because he had to get a job so he could afford to buy his [15¢] lunch at school.

—Rube Boyce, high school coach

I have read so much about guys at school picking on Elvis all the time because of his sideburns and loud clothes, but I don't remember any of these fights. Elvis was a scrapper. No one had to take up for him.

—Farley Guy, high school mate

Elvis came out for the boxing team at Humes....I put him in the ring against Sambo Barrom and this guy bloodied Elvis's nose pretty good. Then Elvis came to me and said, "Coach, I hate to tell you this, but I'm quitting the team. I'm a lover, not a fighter."

—Walt Doxey, high school
boxing coach

I never knew Elvis could sing until someone in my class said Elvis should bring his guitar to our homeroom picnic.

—Elsie Scrivener, Elvis's
twelfth-grade teacher

During our dating days, we had never gone anywhere to dance and it was not until we got to the prom, which was held in the Continental Ballroom of the Hotel Peabody, that Elvis told me he didn't know how to dance. So we sat out the entire evening—never dancing once! Later, I saw him in *Jailhouse Rock* on TV and I thought back to that evening and I said to myself, "I thought he told me he couldn't dance."

—Regis Wilson Vaughn,
Elvis's high school
prom date

I've read a lot of books that say the first time Elvis performed on stage, other than at the Mississippi–Alabama Fair and Dairy Show in 1954...was during his senior year at Humes when he was in a variety show.

That's just not so.

The first time Elvis appeared on stage in Memphis, was during the fall of his junior year at Humes.

—Buzzy Forbes, high school mate

Everyone says that the first recording Elvis did was when he went down to Sun Records and did that record for his mama, but that isn't true.

The first time Elvis's voice was ever recorded was on my fourteenth birthday (September 24, 1950).

My older sister operated a cafeteria over on North Second and that night we had a birthday party there. For my birthday Elvis made up a song and that night he sang it. They had a tape recorder there and recorded the song.

—Doris Guy Wallace,
high school mate

One of the problems we . . . had with Elvis's music at that time was he was known as a hillbilly singer and most of us were just coming out of the big band era. Hillbilly just wasn't our thing during high school. . . . He always seemed to be carrying his guitar with him wherever you saw him; so much so that when we would see other kids carrying guitars, we would laugh and sigh, "Oh, no, not another Elvis!"

—Billie Chiles Turner, high
school mate

We sent him invitations to the Class of '53 reunions in 1968 and 1973, but he never responded to them.

—Georgia Avgeris Scarmoutsos

Memphis Train

If I could find a white man who had the Negro sound and the Negro feel, I could make a million dollars.

—Sam Phillips, president
of Sun Records

Everybody's always saying Elvis Presley was a fuckin' overnight hit. I got news for them. It took a little while.

—Sam Phillips

We…were playing some of the clubs around Memphis. Then along came Elvis. [Bassist, Bill Black] and myself auditioned with him. Sam [Phillips] had a custom record service and Elvis had been in a year before and made a record for his mother. Sam liked his voice and kept his name on file. At the time, the music business was at a very low ebb, and we were all looking for something that would sell. Sam had me get hold of Elvis, and so Elvis came over to my house one Sunday afternoon. We sat around and played, and Elvis sang a little bit of everything—pop, country, R&B. So after that I called Sam and said, "Well, the guy sings good. He doesn't really knock me out, you know, but…" So Sam says, "Let's go into the studio and see what he sounds like on tape." So that's what happened, and the first record came out of that first session.

—Scotty Moore, Elvis's
first guitarist

You want to make some blues?

—Sam Phillips to Elvis

PHILLIPS: What the hell are you doing?
MOORE: We don't know.
PHILLIPS: Better find out fast—and don't lose that sound. Take it from the start again and we'll tape it.

> —Exchange between Sam Phillips and Scotty Moore during Elvis's audition

I recorded [Elvis] and got a moderate response. Elvis did not break overnight. I traveled widely and got encouragement from only two DJs. The white disc jockeys wouldn't play him because he sounded too black, and the black disc jockeys wouldn't play him because he sounded too white.

> —Sam Phillips

If Sam Phillips had been on his toes, he'd have turned the recorder on when that very unrehearsed but talented bunch got to cutting up on "Blueberry Hill" and a lot of other songs. That quartet could sell a million.

> —Robert Johnson, *Memphis Press-Scimitar* columnist, after sitting in on a jam session with Elvis, Carl Perkins, Jerry Lee Lewis, and Johnny Cash

At Sun Studio in Memphis, Elvis Presley called to life what would soon be known as rock and roll with a voice that bore strains of the Grand Ole Opry, Beale Street, of country and the blues. At that moment, he ensured—instinctively knowing—that pop music would never again be as simple as black and white.

> —David Fricke, journalist

Elvis was just an everyday guy—young and wild...He only played rhythm guitar—what I call self-accompaniment. He played a little piano, too. But he didn't consider himself a guitar player as such, but his playing did add to the group, because he played rhythm and more or less tied things together from the rhythm standpoint. But singing was always his first concern.

—Scotty Moore

The first Sun Record we released for Elvis was one of him singing "Blue Moon of Kentucky," which was written and originally released by the bluegrass king himself, Bill Monroe. All we did for Presley's version was give him a rock beat and have him sing the words faster and in a more clipped style. It was a mixture of black rhythm with a white man's country song, and it paved the way for the development of rock and roll.

—Carl Perkins

[Bill Monroe] said, "I want you to hear something," and he had never said anything like that to me before. So, we went up and that's what we heard, "Blue Moon of Kentucky" by Elvis Presley. I believe that was his first number, his first record. I laughed a little bit and everybody else was laughing except Bill. He said, "You better do that number tomorrow if you want to sell some records."...Bill said, "I'm gonna do it next Sunday."

—Carl Stanley of the Stanley Brothers

Like a young boxer after his first professional knockout, Presley is dizzy with the confirmation of his prowess. "Blue Moon of Kentucky" is daring to the point of mania. It is Elvis walking on steel blades, through orange-white flames, invincible with the knowledge he sees in Sam's eyes, hears in his own voice, and feels in his own flushed skin; the knowledge that right now, this moment, he, Elvis Aron Presley is the greatest singer in Memphis and the universe.

—Nick Tosches, rock critic

...He come around, apologized for the way he'd changed "Blue Moon of Kentucky," and I told him that if it would help him get his start and give him a different style, I was for him a hundred percent.

—Bill Monroe

The odd thing about it is that both sides seem to be equally popular on pop, folk, and race record programs. This boy has something that seems to appeal to everybody.

—Marion Keisker of Sun Records, on Elvis's first single, "Blue Moon of Kentucky," backed with "That's All Right"

He never had anything prepared, and the sessions always went on and on...Elvis was different from the other Sun artists who came later. He did not write his own songs. We had to create them on the spot or take somebody else's song from our stable of writers. And he'd never rehearse.... Elvis never had anything ready.

—Marion Keisker

I was afraid to let him sing a rock and roll song on the program, but he said, "They tell me that if I'm going to make any money, I've got to sing rock and roll. What should I do?" I asked him if he needed money, and he said, "I sure do. I've been poor all my life." So I said, "Well, son, go ahead and do what they tell you. Make your money, and then you can sing country music or love ballads or anything you want to sing."

—Country Music Hall of Famer Ernest Tubb, speaking of Elvis's appearance on his "Midnight Jamboree" radio show

Maybe it's ironic that after that first appearance [on the "Grand Ole Opry"] the head of the Opry suggested that Elvis try to find a day job, and that Elvis cried all the way back to Memphis after the Opry show. Then he went on to become the biggest star since Hank Williams. There's some kind of justice in that, I think.

—Hank Williams, Jr.

I set the session for the afternoon, and he came in with pink trousers with blue stripes and he was real nice. He'd "yes sir" and "no sir" you to death.... He was very respectful, a little too much. He was singing and split his pants. One of the boys went out to get him another pair and he threw the split pair in the corner. A girl who was working for the Methodist Publishing Company in the same building asked what to do with the pants, and I told her she better hang on to them, that boy's gonna be famous. She said naw, and six months later there she was on "I've Got a Secret" with Elvis's pants.

—Chet Atkins

Well, son, you're doing all right the way you're going now, so I would just keep it up.

—Vernon Presley to Elvis, on whether Elvis should take the opportunity to sing with the Blackwoods, a gospel group

Follow That Dream

Arguably *the* first rock and roll record, "Rock Around the Clock" was loud, crude, and sexy like nothing we'd heard before—both John [Lennon] and I identified with it almost at once. The only thing wrong with the song...was the singer's image. Bill Haley was fat, married, and utterly conventional in his appearance and demeanor. His watershed hit, it seems, had been something of a fluke.

"Heartbreak Hotel" was something else entirely. After it blasted into our collective consciousness...the youth of Britain—like that of America before it—would never be the same again. Aurally, visually, and unequivocally, Elvis Presley was *the* embodiment of all that "Rock Around the Clock" had merely implied. Elvis *was* rock and roll.

—Pete Shotten, friend of
John Lennon

I didn't think he was as good as the Everly Brothers the first time I ever laid eyes on him.

—Chuck Berry

[1955] was the first year anybody had heard of Elvis. The people there knew something was going on with him because he was stealing the show from everyone. He was on the Hank Snow tour, opening the show at first, but finally they had to put him on last, because all the stars were walking off the tour.

—Phil Everly

Papa, you've heard tell of this Elvis Presley. He's my age, a country boy from Tupelo, a member of the Assembly of God, and was drivin' a truck for a livin' when he comes along an' records a coupla songs an' now he's all over the radio an' teevee. An' I tell you where he got his start—a li'l place in Memphis where I hear anybody can jus' walk in, sit down an' play. Now, what we oughta do is head straightway for Memphis an' talk to the head man 'bout me doin' the same thing as Elvis.

—Jerry Lee Lewis

This cat came out in red pants and a green coat and a pink shirt and socks, and he had this sneer on his face and he stood behind the mike for five minutes, I'll bet, before he made a move. Then he hit his guitar a lick, and he broke two strings. So there he was, these two strings dangling, and he hadn't done anything yet, and these high school girls were screaming and fainting and running up to the stage, and then he started to move his hips real slow like he had a thing for his guitar.

—Bob Lumen, country singer

I was ten when Elvis came along. I used to sing his songs in front of the mirror. I imitated his style, raising the corner of one side of my mouth. I tried to move like him, rotating one leg from the hip. And I tried to comb my hair like him. I used Vitalis, Butch Wax, Brylcream, pulling the comb through my hair and seeing little white globules of grease ooze between the teeth. I dove into a swimming pool, swam the entire length underwater, and surfaced at the other end without a hair out of place.

—Ethan A. Russell,
music reviewer

If you see that guy Elvis Presley tell him we're gonna lock him up, too, cos' he has long hair.

—El Paso sheriff to Little
Richard, after arresting him
for "indecent behavior"

...Elvis had the looks on me. The girls were going for him for more reasons than music. Elvis was hitting them with sideburns, flashy clothes, and no ring on that finger. I had three kids. There was no way of keeping him from being the music...

—Carl Perkins

It was Elvis who, without knowing it, made me a motorcycling fan. I saw a cycle outside Sun Records studio...somebody told me it belonged to Elvis Presley. I finally managed to get to take a cycle ride with the fellow who bought that machine from Elvis and that was the start of it.

—Roy Orbison

I guess everybody in the world tried to be a little like Elvis at the time. There was no way you could compete with him if you were just doing country.

—George Jones, country singer

I don't know what those Presley records have, but I put them on yesterday and the switchboard lit up like Glitter Gulch in Las Vegas. I still can't make out half the words of "Mystery Train" and "I Forgot to Remember to Forget." But the kids seem to get them. He hits them like a bolt of electricity.... My phone hasn't stopped ringing.... Take my word...he's gonna bust wide open into the biggest thing that ever hit the music business.

—DJ Bill Randle of radio station
WERE Cleveland, 1955

Elvis Presley created pandemonium among the teen-age country fans in Jacksonville, Fla., recently, and before he could be rescued from his swooning admirers they had relieved him of his tie, hand-kerchiefs, belt, and the greater part of his coat and shirt.

—*Billboard*, 1955

The first time we met was at a record hop in Cleveland where Elvis was my supporting act. Which was the only time that happened. I never again wanted to follow Elvis. I was very glad I had this big hit record going for me so that when I came on stage it wasn't totally anticlimactic.

—Pat Boone

The first thing I heard when I got back to the States was that Elvis Presley record ["Mystery Train"]. It was a brand-new recording and it just tore me up. I couldn't get it out of my mind. I liked it and for the first time in my life I considered music as my profession.... This Presley sound was something else—like millions of other listeners, I was totally consumed by it....the first time there was an Elvis Presley record, it was an approach and rendition that no other singer had ever done before. It was a brand-new sound, a brand-new feel, it came out of left field. It took this country by storm, and it's hard to describe all those feelings.

> —Conway Twitty, returning to the
> United States after army service
> in Germany

Presley defined rock and roll in 1956. The sneer. The hair. The twisting knees. The thrusting hips. The pink Cadillac.

> —Dick Clark

I was a friend of Elvis's, and I was a fan. I can't say that I went to his concerts and screamed and went all crazy, but maybe it was because I knew him.

> —Brenda Lee

He sings nigger music!

> —Unnamed Nashville music
> executive

...When I came out they weren't playing no black artists on no Top 40 stations, I was the first to get played on the Top 40 stations—but it took people like Elvis, Pat Boone, Gene Vincent, to open the door for this kind of music, and I thank God for Elvis Presley. I thank the Lord for sending Elvis to open that door so I could walk down the road, you understand?

> —Little Richard

I discovered the big secret that would send Elvis to the pinnacle of success. Female entertainers have been using it for years to turn audiences on. I just had Elvis do it in reverse.

—Colonel Tom Parker

I'm sure I'm just one of millions.

—Evelyn Fraser, a fan,
age fourteen

Once he got the money coming in from his records and his concerts, he came back to Humes and he bought the speech teacher some electrical equipment for her class. He bought neckerchiefs and leggings for the ROTC band.

He never bought anything for the athletic department. He said he was going to buy us a washing machine and clothes dryer, but he never did. I don't know why. I guess he probably had other things on his mind and he just forgot.

—Rube Boyce, high school coach

Suspicious Minds

He can't last. I tell you flatly, he can't last.

—Jackie Gleason

Basically, I don't think youth wants this sort of thing.

—Charles Howard Graf, rector of the Protestant Episcopal Church of St. John's in New York

Elvis Presley is a fad, a fellow a girl turns to for one of those mad impetuous infatuations, whereas Perry Como and Eddie Fisher will still be around, the dependable types, when Presley is back driving his truck.

—Unidentified music critic

Elvis is mostly nightmare. On stage his gyrations, his nose-wiping, his leer are vulgar.

—*Look* magazine

Mr. Presley has no discernible singing ability.

—Jack Gould, *New York Times* critic

Extraordinarily untalented.

—John L. Wasserman, San Francisco Chronicle critic

An unspeakably untalented and vulgar entertainer.... Where do you go from Elvis Presley, short of obscenity–which is against the law?

—John Crosby, New York Herald Tribune critic

He can't sing a lick, and makes up for vocal shortcomings with the weirdest and plainly planned, suggestive animation short of an aborigine's mating dance.

—Jack O'Brien, New York Journal-American critic

What's most appalling is the fans' unbridled obscenity, their gleeful wallowing in smut.

—TV Scandals, July 1956

He's just one big hunk of forbidden fruit.

—A fan, explaining why Elvis made her "flip"

I wouldn't let my daughter walk across the street to see Elvis Presley.

—Billy Graham

Elvis Presley is morally insane. The spirit of Presleyism has taken down all the...standards. We're living in a day of jellyfish morality.
—The Reverend Carl E. Elgena,
of Des Moines, Iowa

If the agencies (TV and other) would stop handling such nauseating stuff, all the Presleys of our land would soon be swallowed up in the oblivion they deserve.

—*America: National Catholic Weekly Review*, June 23, 1956

I want to count Elvis's hound dogs twenty years from now. Only time will tell if Elvis is collecting Cadillacs in 1976.

—Spike Jones

We guarantee to break fifty Elvis Presley records in your presence if you buy one of these cars today.

—Sign at a Cincinnati used-car dealer's lot, 1956

It isn't enough to say that Elvis is kind to his parents, sends money home, and is the same unspoiled kid he was before all the commotion began. That still isn't a free ticket to behave like a sex maniac in public.

—Eddie Condon, in *Cosmopolitan*, December 1956

It was beside the point that the gyrating rotary troubadour was seldom if ever heard by an audience screaming like Zulus everytime he moved a muscle. The Pelvis applies more Body English to a song than many a baseball pitcher and he had more movements than a well-oiled Swiss watch.

—*Shreveport Times*

His kind of music is deplorable, a rancid smelling aphrodisiac.

—Frank Sinatra

I applaud the parents of teenagers who work to get the blood and horror gangster stories off TV. They should work harder against the new alleged singer, Elvis Presley.

—Hedda Hopper

The voice is a complete harangue in puffy diction and pure fervency. Under its propulsion the manufactured Folk comes to swarming life like the energetic little creature cavorting in a hunk of rotting ham illuminated by a microscope.

—C. G. Burke, in *High Fidelity*, February 1957

One rock 'n' roll ballad sounded just like the other, and the basic theme and appeal were sex, which Elvis lays on with the subtlety of a bulldozer in mating season.

—*Toronto Daily Star*

We do not tolerate Elvis Presley records at our dances, or blue jeans or ducktail haircuts.

—Orren T. Freeman, principal of Wichita Falls Senior High

I promise that I shall not take part in the reception accorded Elvis Presley and I shall not be present at the program presented by him at the Auditorium on Wednesday, April 3, 1957.

—Oath signed by students of the Notre Dame Convent school in Ottawa (eight girls were later expelled for disregarding their oath.)

Last night's contortionist exhibition at the Auditorium was the closest to the jungle I'll ever get.

—Helen Parmeler, *Ottawa Journal* critic

He strutted like a duck, his hands dangling loosely in front of him. He went to his knees in an attitude of prayer, taking the slender microphone with him. And he finished with a burst of shimmying that left him limp, his thick black hair hanging over his eyes and perspiration pouring down his pancake makeup.

—*Tacoma News Tribune*

The trouble with going to see Elvis Presley is that you are likely to get killed. The experience is the closest thing to getting bashed in the head with an atomic bomb.

—*Detroit Free Press*

Two guys hanging from the balcony railing dropped down into the mob, apparently to get closer to Elvis. One girl kicked an usher in the stomach and they carried him out with the others who had apparently fainted.

—Arlene Cogan, journalist

I wouldn't have Presley on my show at any time.

—Ed Sullivan

♪

Now, ladies and gentlemen, for a second appearance of three appearances on our show tonight, Elvis Presley.

—Ed Sullivan

♪

I want to say to Elvis Presley and the country that this is a real decent fine boy, and we've never had a pleasanter experience on our show with a big name than we've had with you.

—Ed Sullivan

♪

On the Sullivan program he injected movements of the tongue and indulged in wordless singing that were singularly distasteful.... When Presley executes his bumps and grinds, it must be remembered by the Columbia Broadcasting System that even the twelve-year-old's curiosity may be overstimulated.

—Jack Gould, *New York Times* critic

♪

I remember when I was nine years old and I was sittin' in front of the TV set and my mother had Ed Sullivan on, and on came Elvis. I remember right from that time, I looked at her and I said, "I wanna be *just...like...that.*"

—Bruce Springsteen

♪

Elvis Presley ripped off Ike Eisenhower by turning our uptight young awakened bodies around. Hard animal rock energy/beat surged hot through us, the driving rhythm arousing repressed passions.

—Jerry Rubin, political activist
of the 1960s

The performance had not even the quality of true obscenity, merely an artificial and unhealthy exploitation of the enthusiasm of youth's body and mind.
—Dr. Ida Halpern, Vancouver
music critic

It's like having [stripper] Tempest Storm give Christmas presents to my kids.
—Dick Whittinghill, Los Angeles
radio personality, on the release
of *Elvis' Christmas Album*

From a strictly Marxist–Leninist viewpoint, he is a typical example of capitalist exploitation.
Harper's, April 1957

It is sad, but Elvis Presley has more influence on our young people than our educators.
—Jacob Potofsky, president of
the Amalgamated Clothing
Workers of America, comment-
ing on the craze for blue jeans

He's too hot. He can't be maintained at the maximum level.
—Henry J. Saperstein,
concessionaire, shortly after
signing a $26-million deal for
merchandising rights to Elvis

I honestly was not into Elvis. His vibrato annoyed me.
—Neil Sedaka

Country Boy

A lot of people are knocking this Elvis Presley guy. I think he's all right.

—Burl Ives

Elvis Presley was a country boy to start with, and he just kindly put a swivel on his hip and did country music. I like to swing out, but I swing it from the heart. Presley sings it from the hip.

—Roy Acuff

Elvis arrived on the scene when the young needed a romantic image. He filled the bill and on top of that, he can sing.

—Marlene Dietrich

It may surprise you—but I am a Presley fan! Elvis recently saw my folks in California and told them he was a fan of mine—that I had been an inspiration to him....What that boy has done is phenomenal. He has busted many of the disc sales records I held, in little over a year.

—Mario Lanza

He had a pair of $126 gold leather shoes especially made.... He owns more than fifty sports jackets with shoes to match. His current favorite jacket is a $4000 affair, a gold lame creation bedecked with semi-precious stones, jewel encrusted lapels, beaded pocket flaps, and jeweled cuffs. His wrist watch is a $900 job.... yet he had a hole in one of his socks, revealed as he switched shoes!

> —Henry Whiston, in *Melody Maker*

One night I went into the casino after the show and I saw [Bobby Darin] standing there with Elvis Presley; they were probably the two hottest young talents in show business, and both of them were beautiful, polite, talented kids. I thought I'd make them laugh. So I went over to them and I whispered, "I see you fellows are alone. If you need any help meeting some girls, don't be embarrassed to ask me."

Presley thought I was serious. "Thank you, Mr. Burns," he said. Toughest audience I ever worked to.

> —George Burns

I knew that I had never met a more polite, handsome, and unselfish gentleman. He was unspoiled and kind, and he made this [birthday] the most wonderful day of my life. When he left, he gave both [childhood chum Mary Lombardi] and me autographed pictures, and he even asked for my autograph. It was as close to heaven as I could ever imagine feeling.

> —Laurin Chapin, recalling a surprise birthday party given for her by Paramount Studio

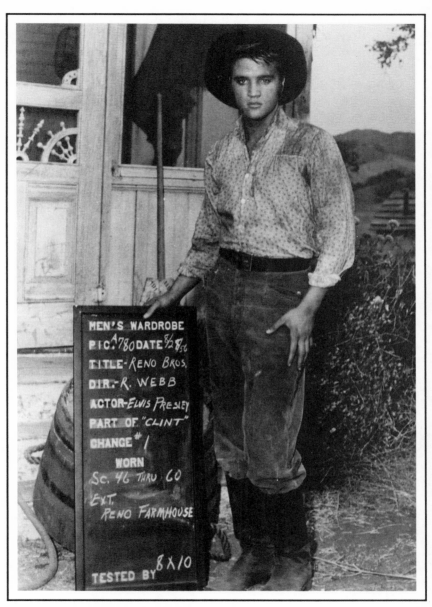

You know, he's a real nice friendly fellow.

—Buddy Holly

Elvis was in the front row on the night Art Rupe came along to hear me. I drew attention to him and he stood up and took a bow. He watched me like a hawk all the way through my act, then afterward there he was waiting for me, a good-looking dude in a white suit with two or three of his boys. After the show he said, "Man, I love your act, you're the greatest."

—Little Richard

Elvis came to my Deer Lake training camp. He told me he didn't want nobody to bother us, he wanted peace and quiet. I don't admire nobody, but Elvis Presley was the sweetest, most humble and nicest man you'd ever meet.

—Muhammed Ali

The best thing Elvis Presley can do for British show business would be to stay away from this country!...From the point of view of our singers doing reasonably well in this country, it is most fortunate that he has not decided to come here. Because after fans had seen the real thing, I'm sure there would be no room for inferior acts, imitators, and many others.

—Bunny Lewis, London agent,
May 12, 1962

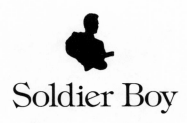

Soldier Boy

GREETINGS: You are hereby ordered for induction into the Armed Forces of the United States and to report at Room 215, 198 South Main Street, Memphis, Tennessee, at 7:45 A.M. on the 20 of January, for forwarding to an armed forces induction station.

> —Elvis's draft notice (Upon arriving, he asked for and got a sixty-day deferral.)

You have shown that you are an American citizen first, a Tennessee volunteer and a young man willing to serve his country when called upon to do so.

> —Telegram from Governor Frank Clement

He sat on his butt in the snow like the rest of us and ate the same crummy food we did, he was a real Joe.

> —An army buddy

I don't think Elvis, especially after he got out of the service, was ever allowed to be Elvis. He lost sight of who he was.

—Brenda Lee

Presley's induction into the military and his transfer to the Federal Republic [West Germany] forced the misuse of rock and roll by NATO forces as a weapon in its "Cold War" that was being waged against the Socialist nations.

—Heinz Hofmann, East German
music critic

Elvis died the day he went into the army. The difference between Elvis and us, is Elvis died and his manager lived. Our manager died and we lived.

—John Lennon

I Want to Be Just Like
Elvis

Once I went all over New York looking for a lavender shirt like the one he wore on one of his albums.

—Paul Simon

I saw a cousin of mine dance when I was very young. She was dancing to Elvis's "Hound Dog" and I have never seen her get up and be moved so much by anything. It really impressed me. The power of music. I started getting records immediately after that.

—David Bowie

I used to tie a rope around the guitar and put it over my neck and play Elvis Presley records real loud, and stand in front of the mirror. I wanted to be Elvis Presley so bad.

—Jesse Ed Davis, rock guitarist

It was definitely Elvis who got me hooked on beat music.

—John Lennon

It was Elvis who really got me hooked on beat music.
—Paul McCartney

I had picked up the guitar because I wanted to be like Elvis Presley

—Paul Simon

The record that made me want to play guitar was "Baby, Let's Play House" by Elvis Presley. I just sort of heard two guitars and bass and thought, "Yeah, I want to be part of this." There was just so much vitality and energy coming out of it.

—Jimmy Page

When I finally realized guitar would be my profession was when I saw Elvis on the Ed Sullivan show.

—Ted Nugent

Elvis was the first *real* person I wanted to be.

—John Waters

Nothing really affected me until Elvis.

—John Lennon

When I first heard Elvis's voice, I just knew that I wasn't going to work for anybody; and nobody was going to be my boss....Hearing him for the first time was like busting out of jail.

—Bob Dylan

I learned to play drums listening to Elvis—beating on tin cans to his records.

—Mick Fleetwood

When I met him, he only had a million dollars worth of talent. Now he's got a million dollars!

—Colonel Tom Parker

♪

If you want to see Elvis Presley, you buy a ticket.

—Colonel Parker to requests for complimentary tickets from people in Elvis's entourage

♪

I consider it my patriotic duty to keep Elvis in the ninety-percent tax bracket.

—Colonel Parker's announced priority as Elvis was inducted into the army

♪

Very few people were lucky enough to find a manager like Elvis Presley had.

—Hank Ballard, country singer/songwriter

♪

Colonel Parker knows more about organizing America than Angela Davis or SDS. He understands the American mentality.

—Phil Ochs, folksinger

♪

"Would $25,000 be all right?"
"That's fine for me. Now, how about the boy?"

—Twentieth Century Fox exec and Colonel Parker, setting up the first movie deal

Hollywood Nights

When Elvis Presley first came to Hollywood to make a movie, he came to see me. He was twenty-one and a millionaire. He had seen James Dean in *Rebel Without a Cause*... and he wanted to know more about Jimmy. We were talking about movies, and he said he didn't see how he could hit the actress who was going to play opposite him. I said, "Just pretend you're slapping at a bothersome fly." But he said, "No, I can't hit a woman!" and I suddenly realized that it wasn't a question of motivation. Elvis actually believed that he had to hit the girl in this scene!

He had to fight another actor, too, he said, but he was in pretty good shape and thought he could take care of him. I explained that you never actually hit anyone in a movie, that it was all faked but the film was cut in such a way as to give the impression that it actually happened. Elvis was angry. He thought I was kidding him; he couldn't accept the fact that he had been deceived all these years by movies.

—Dennis Hopper

...Mr. Presley's first screen appearance...is likely to leave most patrons untouched outside of the sizable circle of the singing guitarist's fans. For the picture itself is a slight case of horse opera with the heaves, and Mr. Presley's dramatic contribution is not a great deal more impressive than that of one of the slavering nags...But one thing you have to say for him—he certainly goes at this job with a great deal more zeal and assurance than the rest of the actors show.

—Bosley Crowther, *New York Times* reviewer, on *Love Me Tender*

Artistically, Elvis grunts his melodies (with a few audible lyrics), studiously shaking his hair over his eyes, whacking his gee-tar and writhing away as if he had just sat down on an anthill.

—Howard Thompson, *New York Times* reviewer, on Elvis's second picture, *Loving You*

...This time most of his singing can actually be understood. And in two numbers, "Treat Me Nice" and the title song, done as a convict jamboree, Elvis breaks loose with his St. Vitus specialty. Ten to one, next time he'll make it—finally getting those kneecaps turned inside out and cracking them together like coconuts. Never say die, El.

—Howard Thompson, reviewing *Jailhouse Rock*

As the lad himself might say, cut my legs off and call me Shorty. Elvis Presley can act. Acting is his assignment in this shrewdly upholstered showcase, and he does it.

—Howard Thompson, reviewing *King Creole*

A very modest man. But then he must have been to perform the way he did. Actually, I'm kidding. Considering he had no training at all, he was remarkably good.

—Walter Matthau, costar in
King Creole

Whatever else the Army has done for Elvis Presley, it has taken that indecent swivel out of his hips and turned him into a good, clean, trustworthy, upstanding American young man. At least, that's the cinematic image projected in the first post-service picture of 1958's most celebrated draftee, the Hal Wallis production, *G.I. Blues*...Gone is that rock 'n' roll wriggle, that ludicrously lecherous leer, that precocious country-bumpkin swagger, that unruly mop of oily hair. Almost gone are those droopy eyelids and that hillbilly manner of speech....Elvis is now a fellow you can almost stand.

—Bosley Crowther

...What really surprised me was the extraordinary talent of Elvis Presley. He took to this part as if he had been a dramatic actor all his life, with a particular feel for Odets' colorful and poetic dialogue.

—Philip Dunne, director, on *Wild in the Country*

The mystery deepens as to what does Elvis Presley do when he isn't actually in front of a camera. Next to Howard Hughes, Elvis is rapidly becoming our leading recluse.

—Louella Parsons, Hollywood columnist

Compared with the Beatles, Elvis Presley sounds like Caruso in *Fun in Acapulco*....And he certainly looks better. In fact, this attractive travel poster for the famed Mexican resort is far and away his best musical feature to date....And Mr. Presley has never seemed so relaxed and personable.

—Howard Thompson

Just send me a million dollars, never mind the script, and Elvis will do the picture.

—Colonel Parker to a Twentieth Century Fox exec negotiating a movie deal

You know, there's strong belief—and judging from what I heard at NBC, I believed it—that when he goes into a room with Colonel Parker, he's one way....I mean, he actually changes. He'll tell you, "Yes, yes, yes," and then he'll go in that room and when he comes out it's "No, no, no."

—Phil Spector

He took appetite suppressants, because he always had a weight problem, especially doing the movies. As you know, a camera will pick up one, two, three, four pounds, whatever and make it look even greater. And so he took appetite suppressants.

—Marty Lacker on Elvis's introduction to drugs

He would sometimes see himself in a movie and he would get disgusted. He would say, "Who's that fast-talking hillbilly sonofabitch that nobody can understand?" One day he is singing to a dog, then to a car, then to a cow. They are all the damned same movies with that Southerner just singing to something different.

—Red West, a member of Elvis's entourage

A Presley picture is the only sure thing in Hollywood.

—Hal Wallis

...This is, after all, just another Presley movie—which makes no use at all of one of the most talented, important and durable performers of our time. Music, youth and customs were much changed by Elvis Presley twelve years ago; from the twenty-six movies he has made since he sang "Heartbreak Hotel" you would never guess it.

—Renata Adler, *New York Times* reviewer, of *Speedway*

These are Elvis pictures.... They don't need titles. They could be
numbered.

—An MGM executive, *Time*

One day someone will actually put Elvis into a good movie, but they
better do it quick before it's too late.

—*Los Angeles Examiner* reviewer
on movie/album *That's the Way
It Is*

Home Sweet Graceland

I was outside working one day, and Mr. Elvis and this other gentleman came walking up to where I was. Mr. Elvis shook hands and said, "How are you, Albert? Is everything all right?"

"Fine, Mr. Elvis. Fine. How are you?"

"Doing just great, Albert."

The other man didn't speak, he just kind of nodded. Mr. Elvis looked at the other man and told him, "You shake hands with him, too. He works for me just like you do."

The other man shook hands with me.

—Albert Clark, handyman at
Graceland for twelve years

I thank God I was able to be there to serve him. I was off only five weeks out of ten years—when I was sick. I had to have a thyroid operation. I did not want to stay away that long. I always felt like Elvis might need me and I was not there.

—Nancy Rooks, Elvis's maid for
seventeen years

One afternoon, he was eating breakfast, and on comes Robert Goulet on the big television set. Very slowly, Elvis finishes what he has in his mouth, puts down his knife and fork, picks up a .22, and—BOOM—blasts old Robert clean off the screen.

—Sonny West, a member of
Elvis's entourage

He loved to throw firecrackers. One day he threw a firecracker in the room where I was. I screamed and he just laughed so hard he cried. He was so much like a little boy.

—Nancy Rooks

He was always up to something, shooting off firecrackers or guns, running around, driving golfcarts and snowmobiles. He'd pull me in a sled and scare me to death. On that long, steep driveway that goes up to Graceland, he'd be pulling me up and falling at the same time. He called me Buttonwood or Yisa. He'd never call me Lisa unless he was mad at me.

—Lisa Marie Presley

[Graceland] is like a graveyard when he's not there. It's just terrible. You can't imagine how everything speeds up when Elvis is there. When he's there that place is full of activity. I've stayed there thirty, forty days at a time. On the other hand, I'd go planning to stay a week and I'd want to leave in two days. It's just such a pace that you couldn't keep up. He wouldn't let you sleep. You're sitting in the living room and fans are there and he's inviting people up from the gate and everyone's having a ball and in awe of Elvis. If one of the people that is staying with Elvis dozes off, he'll shake him and wake him up. If you doze off, brother, you've had it! And you're dying for sleep. Sometimes when he goes to bed and you're settled down in your bed real comfortably and just about to nod off, he decides he can't sleep so he comes down and wakes everybody up and off you go to get a hamburger.

—Eddie Fadal, a member of Elvis's entourage

Git on that damn house phone and call him! Who the hell does that sonofabitch think he is? He ain't no damn better'n anybody else.

—Jerry Lee Lewis to a guard at the Graceland gate

Love Me Tender

Elvis was a great kisser. When we played Spin the Bottle, we always hoped the bottle would land on him.

—Billie Wardlow Mooneyham,
high school mate

I think I'd like to marry him.

—Tuesday Weld

Elvis must have been about twenty and Natalie Wood was eighteen. I'd have about twenty people over, and those two would sit there and neck all evening! Elvis was just mad about her.

—Shelley Winters

Natalie was so crazy about Elvis and we went on the set and visited him. His mommy, Gladys, was always there. He would say, "Mother, give me a sugar." That was when she had to kiss him before he started his scene.... Natalie was a little bit disappointed in Elvis. I don't think he was very bright, he was a good singer. They had matching shirts; Natalie bought them and she bought him presents. But it was boring for Natalie, Mommy being there all the time.

—Maria Gurdin, Natalie Wood's
mother

God, it was awful. He can sing, but he can't do much else.
—Natalie Wood to her sister Lana
after a few days at Graceland,
1957

It's true that at one point we discussed marriage, but we were both very young and for whatever reasons, it didn't work out.

—Ann-Margret

He invited me over to his place after a day filming *Wild in the Country*. I said yes and he said Joe would pick me up at eight o'clock. It was as close to a relaxed family evening as possible. We all just sat around and played card games. Elvis was a friendly host. He made me feel at home.

—Christina Crawford

One girl was here the other day, and after she kissed one of Elvis's shirts hanging in the closet and kissed his bed, she said, "Now I want to kiss Elvis's car," and went outside to his purple Cadillac that was standing in the sun. I told her she'd better watch herself, but she leaned over and kissed the car and jumped away, hollering, "I've burned my lips!" I said, "Well, that ain't nothing to what Elvis's kiss would do to you.

—Gladys Presley, 1956

I dragged one out from under that old pink Cadillac. She must of heard me comin' and hid under there, and all I saw was her feet stickin' out. I said, "Come on out of there," and she didn't move, so I reached down, took ahold of her feet, and pulled. She had a coat of motor oil an inch thick.

—Uncle Travis (Gladys's brother),
Elvis's gatekeeper

My feeling during the show was a total unconsciousness of myself. I was compelled to keep my concentration on him every minute! On a deep level, I was totally "there," but on an unconscious level, I was not there. . . . For days following I was still in a dream world. I remember wanting time to stand still, because as the days went by, I was farther away from Elvis.

—Chloe Lietzke, a fan

I have had only one experience to equal this one, and that is when I gave birth to my children. . . . The fact is, I don't think there was any other person other than Christ himself who could bring about that reaction from a touch of the hand. The warmth was unreal. There was so much love being transmitted from him that it was actually heavenly.

—A Maryland housewife whose hand Elvis once patted

Rock 'n' roll never really had the [fan] loyalty that pop music has. Very few people got that loyalty. One was Elvis Presley, and that's why he was so unique, because he was the only one, really.

—"Little" Anthony Gourdine

He taught me everything; how to dress, how to walk, how to apply makeup and wear my hair, how to return love—his way. Over the years he became my father, husband, and very nearly God.

—Priscilla Presley

He took us both in his arms and held us. . . . We stayed in each other's arms for a long time, caressing our infant and each other. . . . The man in my hospital room that day, was the man I loved, and will always love. . . . He wasn't afraid to show his warmth or vulnerability. He didn't have to act the part of Elvis Presley, superstar. He was just a man, my husband.

—Priscilla Presley

The idea of having sex with a woman who had given birth repulsed him.

—Earl Greenwood, Elvis's cousin and former press agent

You don't know what you're doing. You haven't a clue. What are you doing? Buying people so that your own family can go without? You don't ever look beyond where you are right now.

—Priscilla Presley, complaining of Elvis's extravagance

I realized I couldn't give him the kind of adulation he got from his fans, and he *needed* that adulation desperately. Without it he was nothing.

—Priscilla Presley

No one who worked for Elvis liked Priscilla—no one from Memphis—and it dawned on me that I'd only pretended to like her out of family loyalty.

—Billy Stanley, Elvis's stepbrother

Priscilla Presley…admitted she'd never had caviar in all her years with Elvis because he hated fish and would have thrown her out of the house if he saw her eating any.

—Andy Warhol

Elvis was one of the boys. When you went to one of his parties, the girls usually stayed over to one side of the room and talked girl talk while Elvis surrounded himself with guys and sat around telling stories.

There has been this picture of Elvis as the King of Rock 'n' Roll, with girls hanging on each arm. It's just not so. It was always a bunch of guys standing together in a little group, with Elvis doing his thing. I can only think of one or two instances where the women mingled with the men.

—Wayne Newton

Elvis had animal magnetism. He was even sexy to guys.

—Ian Hunter

Elvis had the kind of magnetism that could derail a marriage.

—Mamie Van Doren

He often wanted his dates to act out roles and play pretend games—a schoolgirl bending over for a spanking and begging for mercy, as he first spanked her, then entered her from behind, or having them act as if they were virgins willing to succumb to his every whim. These power games made him feel strong, superior, and in control—and reinforced his belief that no woman could ever measure up to his mama in purity and goodness. They were all basically whores.

—Earl Greenwood

Presley was doing pictures for Joe Pasternak at MGM. One a day. He'd break just before noon and take a stroll. No bodyguards circled him, because he was on the lot and nobody bothered him. When he got outside, he played Cops and Robbers with some writer. They'd hide behind cars, with their extended fingers, duck, pop up and shoot again. Two little infants. Presley never spoke to this guy, only Cops and Robbers.

Presley would work himself to the two-story building in which some of the TV shows were put together. There was a secretary for one of the companies waiting for him. Next to her would be a girlfriend, a different one each day if possible, and they'd go into a nearby office with a couch and have a quick trio. Then Presley would zip up and head back to his own office. This went on day after day and didn't slow Presley down one second in his close friendships with the three women who were always hanging around, the handful of women who paraded in and out of his portable dressing room near the stage, and whatever female visitors showed up on an afternoon. This was the same Presley who did my show in 1956 when he was eighteen. Offered a wild time by some of the other guests, he passed on it. He had to get his sleep for the show.

—Milton Berle

...Nature had not only endowed Elvis with talent and a beautiful body, but with a tremendous physical sex organ—that throbbed with heat and energy, as I believe no woman has ever experienced.
—Unidentified starlet to Hollywood columnist May Mann

He had to have somebody in bed with him. I don't think sex was even involved a lot of the time. He hated to be alone. If there wasn't a girl there, I'd sometimes sleep at the foot of the bed.
—Rick Stanley

We all heard of the trouble Rob Lowe got into making those sex videos in Atlanta. Well, Elvis beat Rob Lowe to the punch—and that's when I think [Colonel] Parker made his fifty percent deal.

I understand from several...authoritative sources that [the films] still do exist...I'm told that [Parker] has possession of these films. Parker allegedly held them over Elvis's head for many, many years in order to keep him in line.

—Earl Greenwood

Janie even had sex dreams about him.

—Jerry Hopkins, of his wife's enthusiasm for his research for *The Elvis Presley Story*

You that have written books about him, you must remember he has a very pretty little young daughter growing up who is not going to like what is being said about her daddy. I would like to say to her regarding all the bad books written about her father that there is more than enough good to cover up all the bad.

—Nancy Rooks

A Jury of His Peers

Without Elvis none of us could have made it.

—Buddy Holly

Elvis is my man.

—Janis Joplin

Elvis is the greatest blues singer in the world today.

—Joe Cocker

He's a great singer. Gosh, he's so great. You have no idea how great he is, really you don't. You have absolutely no comprehension—it's absolutely impossible. I can't tell you why he's so great, but he is.

—Phil Spector

If there is any hope for a revolution in America, it lies in getting Elvis Presley to become Che Guevara....

—Phil Ochs

I'm crazy about Presley's understanding of what he does.

—Bobby Darin

Elvis was the original punk. I would not have had a musical career without him. In fact, every pop singer or groupy today borrowed from Elvis, and if they say they didn't, they're liars.

—Gary Glitter

I really wish people would stop tryin' to compare me with Elvis. We are entirely different performers. 'Bout the only thing we got in common is that we're from Tennessee. Of course, Elvis has made a lot more money than I have. But, then, he had a three-year start.

—Jerry Lee Lewis

I was salt, and he was pepper. I was a conformist and he was a rebel. I have no doubt that my being in sharp contrast to Elvis actually helped my career.

—Pat Boone

I'm not competing myself against Elvis. Rock just happens to be the media which I was born into.

—John Lennon

...What comes out is not show. There are a lot of people who are good actors at singing so that they make you think they sound good but, with Elvis, he lives it altogether.

—Roy Orbison

He was very polite, but not so cool that it prevents you from making conversation.

—Brian Wilson

I am sure that Presley and the big, bad beat are not so "bad" and will be around forever.

—Doc Pomus, songwriter

I don't know anybody my age that did not sing like him, at one time or another.

—Bob Dylan

To command such a large following, he must be a great performer.

—Paul Anka

Elvis Presley—bloated, over the hill, adolescent entertainer—had nothing to do with excellence, just myth.

—Marlon Brando

He taught white America to get down.

—James Brown

That's my idol, Elvis Presley. If you went to my house, you'd see pictures all over of Elvis. He's just the greatest entertainer that ever lived. And I think it's because he had such presence.

—Eddie Murphy

Elvis Presley was my greatest influence.

—Kyu Sakamoto, Japanese singer

Discount the commercial rubbish he has done often during his career. I just like to think of his trailblazing glorious best, when he sang black man's music in white style and taught the world something about true originality.

—Eric Clapton

You know, of course, that [Roy Orbison] was Elvis Presley's favorite singer.

—Duane Eddy

When he started, he couldn't spell Tennessee. Now he owns it.

—Bob Hope

About a year ago (1976), we met in Memphis at the airport....He said, "Where you going?" I said, "I'm going to Orlando." He said, "Man, that's the wrong direction. But then, you were always going the wrong way, weren't you?" We...laughed, and I said, "Well, Elvis, that all depends on where you're coming from."

—Pat Boone

There have been contenders, but there is only one King.

—Bruce Springsteen

Something very nice happened, and the Beatles got a great kick out of it. We just received a wire...from Elvis Presley and Colonel Tom Parker wishing them a tremendous success in our country. I think that was very nice.

—Ed Sullivan

...What a total anticlimax *he* was. He seemed to be completely out of his head. Either he was on pills or dope, or else acting unbelievably blasé—whatever it was, he was just totally uninterested and uncommunicative.

—John Lennon on the Beatles' being
introduced to Elvis

All this hollerin' an' screamin' ain't nothin' new. And it ain't nothin' to what it was when Elvis and me started it.

—Jerry Lee Lewis on the reception
the Beatles got in America

The Singer and His Songs

[Elvis's] neighbors were the people who drove trucks and worked in gas stations and spent their youth in roadside taverns listening to tales of their heartbreak hotel. Their life was an Elvis song.

—Robert Carey, in the *Commercial Appeal*, August 1977

His range is greater than that of almost any other popular singer. His voice is a mellow and expressive instrument.

—Henry Edwards, in *High Fidelity*, November 1972

I felt wonderful when he sang "Bridge Over Troubled Water," even though it was a touch on the dramatic side, but so was the song.

—Paul Simon

...Elvis plays a fairly good rhythm guitar, and he'll surprise you sometimes. He'll pick up an electric guitar and sit down and play some blues.

—James Burton, guitarist

I liked Elvis Presley. Elvis Presley recorded a song of mine. That's the one recording I treasure the most...it was called "Tomorrow Is a Long Time." I wrote it but never recorded it.

—Bob Dylan

He would not look at a song before I had seen it first, which didn't mean that I would pick them, I would just screen them for him, and then out of those that I had screened, he would make his own selections.

—Freddie Bienstock, music
publisher

...Elvis produced his own records. He came to the session, picked the songs, and if something in the arrangement was changed, he was the one to change it. Everything worked out spontaneously. Nothing was really rehearsed. Many of the important decisions normally made previous to a recording session were made during the session. What it was, was a look at the future. Today everybody makes recordings this way. Back then, Elvis was the only one. He was the forerunner of everything that's record production these days.

—Bones Howe, recording engineer
and record producer

[It was] the finest music of his life. If there was ever music that bleeds, this was it. Nothing came easy that night and he gave everything that he had—more than anyone knew he had.

—Greil Marcus, of Elvis's
1968 NBC-TV special

They ruined it; you should have seen it before they edited it. I didn't see the final version. What was originally done was sensational. How it ended up I can't tell you. I mean they cut out everything that was Elvis, *really* Elvis. They destroyed a lot of it, so I can't tell you how the final version was. But I think he's a sensation on stage.

—Phil Spector, on the 1968
NBC-TV special

The performance he gave us was a spectacular triumph of insight into the mind of our mindless era. No demagogue of fact or legend has ever seen more keenly into the blackest depths of his followers or grasped them in so many ways. He knows what ails and uplifts us, he rubs each of our dirtiest little secrets until it shines brightly in the dark, hollow arena of our souls.

—*New York* magazine on Elvis's
Madison Square Garden kickoff
for his 1972 tour

Not Wanted by the FBI

Presley's sincerity and good intentions notwithstanding, he is certainly not the type of individual whom the director would wish to meet. It is noted at the present time he is wearing his hair down to his shoulders and indulges in the wearing of all sorts of exotic dress.

> —Reaction from J. Edgar
> Hoover's office to prospect of
> a visit from Elvis

Morris observed that he has known Presley for many years, that despite his manner of dress, he is a sober, clean-minded young man who is good to his family and his friends and who is very well regarded by all, including the law enforcement community in the Memphis, Tennessee, area where he was raised and still resides.

> —Internal FBI memo citing
> Shelby County sheriff W. N.
> Morris on Elvis's character

Presley indicated that he is of the opinion that the Beatles laid the groundwork for many of the problems we are having with young people by their filthy unkempt appearances and suggestive music while entertaining in the country during the early and middle 1960's. He advised that the Smothers Brothers, Jane Fonda, and other persons in the entertainment industry of their ilk have a lot to answer for in the hereafter for the way they have poisoned young minds by disparaging the United States in their public statements and unsavory activities.

> —From an FBI memo after Elvis's
> visit there (but not to see the
> director)

65

Boy, you sure do dress kind of wild.

> —Richard Nixon, on Elvis's White
> House visit

President Elvis Presley, Memphis S, Tennessee
You will be nest [sic] on my list. 1. Elvis Presley   2. Johnny Cash
3. Tommy Moese   4. President LBJ   5. George C. Wallace

> —Death threat received from
> Huntsville, Alabama, January
> 1964

Despite his rather bizarre appearance, Presley seemed a sincere, serious minded individual who expressed concern over some of the problems confronting our country, particularly those involving young people....He said that he spends as much time as his schedule permits talking to young people and discussing what they consider to be their problems with him. Presley stated that his long hair and unusual apparel were merely tools of his trade and afforded him access to and rapport with many people particularly on college campuses who considered themselves "anti-establishment."

> —FBI memo

Viva Las Vegas

Elvis participates in a one on one relationship with his audience, and when he steps on stage it is he and he alone who is the subject of the manic, uncontrolled, irrational adulation which is the core of the American star system.

—Jon Landau

I was in his dressing room, and it was the most beautifully emotional thing I have ever seen between two men. The Colonel came down after show time into the room. He just said, "Where is he?" The Colonel had tears in his eyes. His face was twisted in emotion. I had never seen him like that before.... Elvis came out. The Colonel took one step forward and so did Elvis. There were no words, they just put their arms around each other in a big hug. The Colonel had his back to me and I knew it was a private thing where we shouldn't hang around. We excused ourselves. But the Colonel's body was shaking with emotion. It was a beautiful moment.

—Charlie Hodge, Las Vegas Hilton

Elvis has changed the whole economy of Las Vegas. Business was way off, and when Elvis Presley is posted on the marquee, it's instant S.R.O.! People from all over the world come and fight for admittance during his engagement. Chartered planes bring his fans from as far as France, Japan, and Australia.... Elvis is a phenomenon!

—Spokesman for International Hotel, on Elvis's first Las Vegas engagement

When Elvis Presley appears in concert, one of the major excitements is his isolation from his audience. No one would want to think of Elvis leaning over to one of his screaming female fans and confessing that he is not very different from any other male, that he eats, shits, screws and worries about losing his hair. But no one would think twice about a Seeger or a Don McLean stepping out and telling his audience, I am just like you, the same idiocies anger me and the same problems plague me.

The advantage of the Elvis method is that he rarely needs to expose himself; he can easily hide behind the character created by his managers and the media.

—Bob Sarlin, journalist

In his heyday, when he was really hot, there was an explosion of energy between Elvis and his audience. I wasn't a wild fan of Elvis's, but put the man onstage doing his music, and you got something more powerful than the sum of its parts. You got magnetism in action. Maybe it was sexual, I don't know, but if ever a performer could get up onstage and turn a crowd into crashing waves of energy, it was Elvis.

Yet Elvis couldn't really whip up a Las Vegas dinner-show crowd on a regular basis. I went to see Elvis one night on the Strip and I...thought: What is going on here? There was Elvis up there working his ass off, and the crowd was just kind of politely exhausted. They clapped and whistled, but you couldn't feel them giving anything back. I felt like jumping on top of a table and yelling, "Hey everybody, that's Elvis Presley up there! You should be jumping up screaming."

—Willie Nelson

He was just as important to Vegas as he was to the hotel. It was like bringing in a major convention. Everybody reaped the benefits. His August 1973 engagement was his last full month in Vegas. He was doing two shows a day for twenty-eight days. That's 100,000 people a month. We've never seen anything like it and probably never will again.

—Bruce Banke, public relations executive for the Las Vegas Hilton

He came down and sat at the dinin' room table. He said, "Where is it?" I gave it to him. He slipped it on his finger and looked at it and said, "God, won't Sammy Davis, Jr., shit a brick when he sees this."
—Lowell Hays, on a $55,000 ring
he designed for Elvis

It's Elvis at his most indifferent, uninterested and unappealing. He's not just a little out of shape, not just a bit chubbier than usual, the Living Legend is fat and ludicrously aping his former self....It is a tragedy, disheartening and absolutely depressing to see Elvis in such diminishing stature.
—*The Hollywood Reporter,* on
Elvis's 1973 Vegas show

[My wife] Leba and I went to see Elvis Presley at the Hilton, and although he was bloated and obviously in trouble with his life, he put on a big show. At one point Elvis stopped in the middle of a song and said, "Excuse me, I have to go to the bathroom." The show went right on; he was smart enough to know that he now required a whole stageful of musicians to back him up. Elvis was a caricature of his former self and it was sad to see a legendary star falling apart before our eyes.
—Neil Sedaka

The last time he sang in Las Vegas he telephoned and said, "You haven't been over, Chief," so I said okay and went to see his show. But I didn't want to go because I loved my friend and didn't want to see his decline....It was obvious to me that this was Elvis's swan song because practically every song he sang was a way of saying good-bye: "My Way." "Lord, This Time You Gave Me a Mountain," "Just a Closer Walk With Thee." He must have done nine of these songs. He was saying good-bye to the world. Anyone who was tuned in had to realize he had had it.
—Wayne Newton

The fact that he was still doing it at all, getting up there and giving out that much energy per show, is amazing. Whether he was overweight or wearing white suits or whatever was superficial compared to the fact that he was doing it.

—Lindsey Buckingham

He told us his problems, and we told him ours, which was another burden he carried. We just heard one guy's problems, and he heard everybody's. And he was such a good person that he just wanted to try and alleviate everybody's problems.... Toward the end, he couldn't carry everybody's load anymore. He lived under a lot of pressure.

—Marty Lacker, Elvis's cousin and a member of his entourage

The King Is Dead

My partner and I had been called to a real tough neighborhood because of a domestic dispute. When we got there, this couple was just about to kill each other. The woman had the man down and was choking him. We pulled them apart....Just then, it came over our walkie-talkie unit that Elvis had died. The woman started crying and the man went limp....This seemed to take their attention from their fight and they went to watching TV and talking about Elvis. It was real strange. We left and didn't hear anything more from them that night.

—Curt Willis, Shelby County
deputy sheriff

Although I predict that 1976 is going to be a new beginning for Elvis Presley, in the long run he is doomed, his inside outside battle will rage more and more without him being able to gain control, his greatest hope for salvation rests in his actions to get the proper psychological help now.

—Count John Manolesco,
astrologer

August 16, 1977. I was actually sick—I had a cold when my dad came down and said: "I have some bad news for you." I said, "What?" He said, "Elvis died." I'll never forget that.

—Paul Hipp, actor

Why in the world would my Elvis records melt on the day he died?
—Ruth Ann Bennett

I broke down…One of the very few times. I went over my whole life. I went over my whole childhood. I didn't talk to anyone for a week after Elvis died. If it wasn't for Elvis and Hank Williams, I couldn't be doing what I do today.
—Bob Dylan

I know that Elvis had a strong faith, but it was just that there was no one close to him that loved him enough to tell him what he was doing to himself.
—Roy Orbison

I just can't believe he's dead. But I just thank God that Elvis died here at Graceland instead of on the road just like any other rock 'n' roll singer.
—An unnamed fan

Makes you feel sad, doesn't it? Like your grandfather died.…Yeah, it's just too bad it couldn't have been Mick Jagger.
—Malcolm McLaren

I thought he died when I recorded "Heartbreak Hotel."
—John Cale of the Velvet Underground

I was glad. Just another one outa the way. I mean, Elvis this, Elvis that. All we hear is Elvis. What the shit did Elvis do except take dope that I couldn't git ahold of? That's very discouraging, anybody that had that much power to git ahold of that much dope. All I did was drink whiskey.

—Jerry Lee Lewis

I went to Graceland that night. The crowds had already started gathering around the gate. Some agents from the Tennessee Bureau of Investigation put me in one of their cars and got me in without anybody seeing. I saw Priscilla and his daughter, and I saw one of his aides who's been a good friend of mine for sixteen years. I talked to Elvis's father, saying what I could to help console him. But when I walked over to the open casket, I needed consoling. I put my hand over his heart and said with tears in my eyes, "You rat; why'd you leave me?"

—Roy Orbison

For some reason his death hit me very hard. We were a lot alike in many ways—both poor boys from the country raised on gospel and R 'n' B. "Hound Dog" and "Please" both came out the same year. He had lived in Hollywood a long time and then like me, had moved back home to try to preserve himself. Somehow or another he just didn't manage to do it. They kept him shut away all the time; he couldn't get out and be with the people. I knew he was a poor boy and never intended to go that way. When you're poor, you have survival on your mind.

—James Brown

He was a troubled young man; he was a troubled middle-aged man. I guess he was troubled most of his life.

—George Nichopoulos, M.D.,
Elvis's personal physician

Fuckin' good riddance to bad rubbish. I don't give a fuckin' shit, and nobody else does either. It's just fun to fake sympathy, that's all they're doin'.

—Johnny Rotten

The news of his death absolutely stunned me. I stopped drinking.
—Elton John

Great move, public relationswise.

—Unnamed publicist on hearing of Elvis's death

There have been many accolades uttered about his talent and performances through the years, all of which I agree with wholeheartedly. I shall miss him dearly as a friend.

—Frank Sinatra

A lot of [Elvis's pain] was self-inflicted. I knew him very well. He always felt that somebody was after him. When you have that kind of fear, that kind of attitude, you attract people who want to do you harm.

—Liberace

Elvis is a classic example of the celebrity running headlong away from reality. His whole world eventually was bordered by the insides of some of those hotels he stayed in for months at a time. His world was right there inside those walls and that was the way he wanted it. Entertainers like that are wide open to exploiters who want to take advantage of them.

—Conway Twitty

How do you protect a man from himself?

—Dave Hebler, former
Elvis bodyguard

I met him when I was ten but never saw him again. We were born less than thirty miles apart in Mississippi. I idolized him as a performer. The last year he was alive, he played a concert near my home in Florida, and I happened to be off that week. I felt a real urgency to see that show and to get backstage to meet him. It was sold out of course, and when I contacted a member of his entourage, he was so pompous about *trying* to get me in I just let it drop, thinking there would be other opportunities. But a few months later Elvis was dead and I regretted so much that I had let a rude flunky prevent me from seeing him....I believe Elvis's biggest problem was some of the group he had around him. They cut him off from the real world.

—Tammy Wynette

I was a Beatles baby. I was seven when they came on, and Elvis was completely old hat. He was the older generation. When I was a student at the University of Alabama, he came to give a concert, and I could have paid one dollar to hear him and I didn't. Of course, I could kick myself now, but he was old, fat and irrelevant, and I literally didn't walk across the street to see him. None of my friends did either.

—Mark Childress, author

Whereas Elvis Presley was an inspiration to all by showing that through hard work and dedication we can make the world a better place in which to live; and whereas Elvis Presley's sudden and untimely death shocked and saddened the world on August 16, 1977. Now therefore I, Lamar Alexander, as Governor of the State of Tennessee, do hereby proclaim August 16, 1979, as Elvis Presley Day.

—Formal proclamation declaring
a commemorative holiday for
Elvis

I can see now why Elvis killed himself with drugs and why so many people have turned to drugs and committed suicide. Because it can really, really get to you if you're alone. Thank God we have each other.

—Jordan Knight, of New Kids on the Block

When they celebrated the tenth anniversary of Elvis Presley's death, it was more like a canonization. People lined up to visit Graceland. Middle-aged women—and yes, men, too—with tears in their eyes. I couldn't believe one woman saying, "Elvis's death meant more to me than a death in my own family."

—Kirk Douglas

We must immediately make sure that outsiders cannot exploit the name of Elvis Presley. We can mourn, but a long and inactive period of grief over Elvis will prove disastrous for you, for his daughter, for his estate, for his legend. . . . His death doesn't change anything. If you show signs of weakness at this moment everything will fall apart.

—The Colonel to Vernon Presley after hearing of Elvis's death

I'll keep right on managing him.

—Colonel Parker, on being asked what he would do now that Elvis was dead

You Don't Know Me

You won't probe too deeply, will you?
> —Elvis's publicist to journalist William Offerburnhill prior to a 1969 interview

Well, Jesus H. Christ, it's obvious. The son of a bitch died of drugs.
> —Baptist Hospital pathologist remarking on lab tests of Elvis's blood

The coroner's report stated that Elvis died of a heart attack and that he had an enlarged heart. This was no surprise to me. Elvis had the biggest heart of anyone I've ever known. He was both generous and compassionate, and his love for people was tremendous. Thus this seems the appropriate way for him to have gone. In my opinion, he had one other fatal illness—loneliness.
> —Marian Cocke, Elvis's private nurse

"The Kit" went everywhere with Elvis, and I was the guy designated to take care of it. If he went out for a drive, that meant I brought the kit. It had all kinds of uppers—Dexedrine, Black Beauties. Then you've got the Class A Percodan, Demerol, codeine. There were barbiturates—Tuinal, Seconal, Nembutal, Carbital. Toward the end there was liquid Demerol. Needles. Plus he had money inside the kit—ten grand in a wallet—makeup, a driver's license, and a lot of jewelry.
> —Rick Stanley

People here in the business knew long before it became common knowledge about Elvis Presley's drug habits; the maids who cleaned the rooms following his last attempt to record here [he never made it out of the hotel] reported huge piles of junk-food containers and used syringes left behind. This was never reported in the press, however.

—John Lomax III, music writer

All the traces that might point to the real horror of Elvis or confirm that this was no accident were removed. Nobody thought it was strange. It was just the thing we had always done. Elvis had lived a lie and now he had died a lie.

—David Stanley

No, I don't think he had anything there to OD on. He had taken a couple of sleeping pills or he was given a couple of sleeping pills. Whether he had taken them or not, I don't know. And the only other medicines he had on hand was some medication he used for his colon and medication he used for his sinus.

—Dr. George Nichopoulos

The official investigation of the death of Elvis Presley, at least insofar as we have been able to determine, must rank among the worst, most unprofessional investigations of this type ever made. For whatever reason or motive, essentially no real effort was ever made to truly unearth the circumstances of Elvis Presley's death. It seems almost as if the city of Memphis itself just did not care to know the truth about the death of its most prominent citizen.

—Geraldo Rivera, in lead-in to a "20/20" investigation of Elvis's death

I not only place [responsibility for Elvis's death] on the doctors, but I place it on the people around him, too. They contributed to it. I think people like Colonel Tom Parker should not have allowed him to work when they became aware of his problems. If you notice the disintegration of Elvis Presley in the last three or four years—his weight problem, he almost collapsed on his last concert when he came off the stage.

What are we talking about? We're talking about a money machine. They should have taken action. Allegedly they love him. Everybody. Every time you read an article, they say, "I was devoted to Elvis. The greatest man that ever lived." You can't be devoted, take his money and watch him kill himself.

—John O'Grady, Los Angeles Police Department officer and friend

In accordance with interpretations made by our consultants versed in therapeutic and toxic drug levels in body fluids and tissues, and in accordance with our interpretation of results on drug levels and their clinical significance as recorded in the literature, it is our view that death in the case of Baptist Hospital A77-160 resulted from multiple drug ingestion [commonly known as "polypharmacy"].

—Pathologists' conclusion contained in the suppressed autopsy report, made public as a result of the "20/20" investigation

Long Live the King

Marion unlocked the door and we went inside. Right away we noticed that the structure of Elvis which stands on the coffee table in front of the sofa had fallen to the floor and broken. Then we saw that our two favorite pictures of Elvis had fallen from the mantle over the fireplace and the glass in the frames had shattered.... There was no sign that anyone had come into the house. All the windows and doors had been locked.... We talked for a while about what might have happened. By then it was six o'clock. I turned on the television set to get the news, and the first thing we heard was that Elvis had died.

—Arthur Parker

He said, "Are you satisfied with your life, Missy?"... That question hit me like the proverbial ton of bricks.... I said, "You're a better psychologist than I am, and you've never been to school." As soon as I made that remark, and even as the thought had come to me, I felt embarrassed and ashamed of myself, as though I had come across as condescending to him. But he smiled, and he... said, "I've been to the *best* school." And from the way he said it, I knew immediately he was right. After all, he had *died*....

—Hilda Weaver, clinical psychologist, on a visitation in November 1977

As Jennifer was dying, she seemed to light up....She smiled a big smile. Jimmy and I were hugging her and crying and she tried to sit up in bed. She said, "Love you Mommy and Dimmy." Then she said, "Here comes Elvis."...Then she collapsed and died.

> —Sherry Reed, on the death of her ten-year-old retarded daughter

Elvis's death rattled me personally. I became very anxious....I worried about my health all the time for maybe six months....The jacket Elvis gave me started acting up around that time. Twice within a week the jacket fell to the floor of the closet while I was at work. Never in all the time I had it did it fall, and then it fell twice in a week....It was in November that the jacket really got active. It fell off the hanger three times in early November, once when I was looking straight at it....Then on November 20, 1977, I woke up in the middle of the night....The closet was open on the side the jacket was in....The jacket sleeve was moving, bending all the way up and then back down. I was petrified.

> —Janice McMichael, on a jacket Elvis had given her

When I finally realized that Jeremy was Elvis, he was almost eighteen months old. One day I was playing with him and I noticed something about his eyes. They were exactly like Elvis's....So I looked right into Jeremy's eyes and I said, "Jeremy, are you Elvis?" He laughed and I'm sure he knew what I was talking about. He said, "Uh-huh" and nodded his head yes....Ever since that day I have known in my heart that Jeremy is Elvis.

> —Nancy Morgan

You don't really believe that Elvis is dead, do you?

—Charles Lassiter

When they wheeled me into the delivery room, they put this mask on me and I breathed the anesthetic. . . . The doctors and nurses were all around me in these white gowns, looking at me. Right there among them, Elvis Presley appeared. He smiled and winked at me. He said, "Relax, Bess, it's O.K. I'll be here with you.". . . I stared into his face, then I would blink or look away, but when I looked back he was still there. . . . Then, when the baby came, it was he who said, "It's a boy!" For an Elvis Presley fan, there can't be a bigger thrill than hearing Elvis himself telling you you have a new baby.

—Bess Carpenter

Elvis, Inc.

Now there are those who think a hundred Elvis Presley look-alikes singing "Jailhouse Rock," "Don't Be Cruel," and "Blue Suede Shoes" for a manufactured event in a sterile football palace was somehow, well, tacky.

So let 'em. Elvis would have loved this. Absolutely loved it. And that's good enough for me.

—David Hinckley, New York *Daily News* writer

Thirteen years after his death, Elvis is bigger than ever. Elvis clones appear by the dozens on stage, screen, and television, and the man himself (if you believe the tabloids) has been seen in a Michigan supermarket and even on Mars. What's more, Elvis is worth more dead than alive. Last year his estate earned more than $15 million from sales of records and souvenirs and from the 500,000 adoring fans who lined up to take guided tours of Graceland.

Not even Elvis could kill Elvis.

—Albert Goldman, Elvis biographer

Presley and his image or likeness are trademarks. You think of him as a dead public figure, but he's really a living business.

—Mark Childress

The earth contained in the attached packet was removed from the yard of Elvis Presley. This is actual soil from his home, Graceland, in the City of Memphis, and the State of Tennessee.

—Inscription on a packet of soil
sold in the Graceland gift shop

No one has ever lost money on Elvis Presley.

—Vester Presley

[The medium] just went into a trance, a very deep trance. Elvis Presley apparently came to her, used her. . . . She was speaking in his words; she sang the song in his voice. He sang about how sorry he was that he defiled his body, that he couldn't do what God had wanted him to do on this earth and gave him the talent to do. Because he had defiled his body he couldn't reach the people he wanted to reach, the people who were his followers or just liked to hear him.

While she was singing her face changed. Her nose changed. It turned white and became Elvis Presley's nose, in order to reach the tone that he would sing in. Her nasal quality had to change because Elvis sang in falsetto, which I believe must have come from his nose or that area someplace. He sang very beautifully when he sang falsetto. Her nose changed into a sculptured Elvis Presley nose in front of my eyes.

—Arthur Myers

The Wonder of You

Among the countless clichés Elvis embodied, "living legend" is the most perfectly realized.

—Dave Marsh

...two thousand years from now they'll still be hearing about Elvis Presley.

—Wolfman Jack

The fact that someone with so little ability became the most popular singer in history says something significant about our cultural standards.

—Steve Allen

I don't think that Elvis let anybody down. Personally, I don't think he owed anything to anybody. I think that, as it was, he did more for most people than they'll ever have done for them in their lives. The trouble that he ran into, that's the trouble that you run into. It's hard to keep your head above the water, but sometimes it's not right for people to judge the way that they do.... I don't think Elvis sold out when he lived in Graceland—people never sold out by *buying* something. It wasn't ever something they bought; it was something they *thought* that changed....

—Bruce Springsteen

What was new about Elvis Presley was not that he caused riots (Sinatra had done the same), but that this country singer who once used to hang around the black areas of Memphis was, in those celebrated words of Sun Records' boss, Sam Phillips, "a white man with the Negro sound and the Negro feel."

—Robin Denselow, British
rock critic

Before Elvis, rock had been a gesture of vague rebellion. Once he'd happened, it immediately became solid, self-contained. . . . it spawned its own style in clothes and language and sex, a total independence in almost everything. . . . This was the major breakthrough, and Elvis triggered it. . . . he became one of the people who have radically affected the way other people think and live.

—Nik Cohen, music critic

He never contributed a damn thing to music.

—Bing Crosby

Elvis was a hero to most,
but he didn't mean shit to me.
—Chuck D, of Public Enemy

There's no way to measure his impact on society or the void that he leaves. He will always be the King of Rock 'n' Roll.

—Pat Boone

Elvis had been our king, our musical ambassador, our assurance that the American dream could come true. When he died he took some of our hope with him.

—"Cousin" Bruce Morrow,
WABC-New York radio
personality

Elvis had the power over people's imaginations that would enable him to obtain high office.

—Richard Nixon

Elvis Presley's death deprives our country of a part of itself. His music and his personality fusing the styles of white country and black rhythm and blues, permanently changed the face of American popular culture. His following was immense, and he was a symbol to the people the world over of the vitality, rebelliousness, and good humor of this country. Elvis may be gone, but his legend will be with us for a long time to come.

—Jimmy Carter

Presley in fact remains the quintessential symbol and creation of the rock 'n' roll revolution: physically attractive, unashamedly erotic in his music and his performance (who can forget Elvis's gyrating pelvis?), naturally heroic and priestly in stature, musically talented and stylistically archetypal, and yet continually on the edge of musical disaster.

—Richard Middleton, music critic

Elvis Presley's music was thrilling because it dissolved the signs that had previously put adolescence together. He celebrated—more sensually, more voluptuously than any other rock 'n' roll singer—the act of symbol creation itself.

—Simon Frith

Presley's appeal did not derive solely from his musical abilities; several of his competitors were also remarkably talented, and a few of them, such as Charlie Rich, Carl Perkins, and Jerry Lee Lewis, were probably more adept at re-creating black styles than was Elvis. Along with talent and energy, Elvis brought a sexual charisma into the music business that his colleagues did not possess. Certainly no country entertainer before him had exhibited such raw masculine appeal.... Elvis was the first of a myriad of youthful entertainers who won large followings as much for their youth and vitality as for their talent.

> —Bill C. Malone, country music historian

I think deep down Elvis never worried about anybody catchin' or passin' him. But he certainly never acted like he was a big cock o' the walk.... He was very humbled by the fact that he was risin' so fast. He didn't know what was happening, but he took it and handled it very well. I think he lasted under the pressure longer than any of us could have.

> —Carl Perkins

He was a precious gift from God
We cherished and loved him dearly.

He had a God-given talent that he shared
with the world. And without a doubt,
He became the most widely acclaimed,
capturing the hearts of young and old alike.

He was admired not only as an entertainer,
but as the great humanitarian that he was:
for his generosity, and his kind feelings
for his fellow man.

He revolutionized the field of music and
received its highest awards.

He became a living legend in his own time,
earning the respect and love of millions.

God saw that he needed some rest and
called him home to be with him.

We miss you, son and daddy. I thank God
that he gave us you as our son.

TCB

By Vernon Presley

—The inscription on Elvis's
headstone

Elvis, we came by to see you, but you were gone. You left on tour with our Lord, we know. Here within our hearts always and ever we love only you, your smile, the sparkle in your eyes, how can we forget? We didn't come to say goodbye, until we climb these golden stairs, let's just say until we meet again.

Elvis, your star will always shine, we miss you... you have only just begun to live.

There has been only two people upon their departure who have moved the world so much, Jesus Christ, Our Lord, and Elvis, the king.

Elvis, you lived "The Impossible Dream."

We are proud that the greatest person in the world came from the South.

To the King: You are the Lord's answer to freedom.

Elvis, I came too late!

—Graffiti from the walls of Graceland

He was very much the same the last time I saw him and the first time I saw him.... He never changed; he just polished what he started with. But he always had *it*.

—Carl Perkins

There's just no way to explain it. It was brand-new—the very first. That was it. People can trace it to Bill Haley, or Bo Diddley, or a few other singers of the day. But it was Elvis and no one else. He was the one. Nothing like it. Period. He bowled people over. He changed the whole damn world.

—Conway Twitty

I hope people remember the impact—it's not only historical fact, but it's definitely lingering fact.

—Roy Orbison

I think Elvis Presley will never be solved.

—Nick Tosches, rock critic

Elvis will remain the founder of rock-and-roll in most people's minds, and every rock singer owes something to him in the matters of inflection and visual style. The Beatles and Bob Dylan brought the music closer to art as it has been traditionally defined. But Elvis was and remained a working-class hero, a man who rose from obscurity and transformed American popular art in answer to his own needs— and who may possible have been destroyed by the isolation that being an American celebrity sometimes entails. He was as much a metaphor as a maker of music, and one of telling power and poignancy.

—John Rockwell, *New York Times* critic

I don't think Elvis could have become the performer and man he was if that momma's boy thing were true.

—Wayne Newton

98

He was ahead of his time because he had such deep feelings. He had the privilege of deep feelings because he was deeply loved by his mother, Gladys. He was able to appreciate profound beauty in sounds. And he started a musical revolution. They say all revolutions start from love.

—Imelda Marcos

I believe I will see Elvis Presley in Heaven.

—Billy Graham

Elvis had the wisdom that makes wise men foolish.

—Bono

The King is gone, but his look is not forgotten.

—*Details* magazine lead-in for a
December 1990 fashion spread

I'd like to resurrect Elvis. But I'd be so scared of him I don't know whether I could *do* it.

—John Lennon

That Elvis, man he's all there is. There ain't no more. Everything starts and ends with him.

—Bruce Springsteen

Elvis is dead.
Elvis is dead.
Elvis is dead.
Elvis is dead.
Elvis is dead.

—Living Colour

Elvis Presley was an explorer of vast new landscapes of dream and illusion. He was a man who refused to be told that the best of his dreams would not come true, who refused to be defined by anyone else's conceptions.

This is the goal of democracy, the journey on which every prospective American hero sets out. That Elvis made so much of the journey on his own is reason enough to remember him with the honor and love we reserve for the bravest among us. Such men made the only maps we can trust.

—Dave Marsh

Index

Sandra Choron and Bob Oskam are New York-based book producers who have written eight books between them, mostly on popular culture. They are among the King's most loyal subjects.